Fact Finders™

Energy at Work

Geothermal Power

by Josepha Sherman

Consultant:
Roland N. Horne
Professor and Chairman
Stanford Geothermal Program
Stanford University, California

Capstone
press
Mankato, Minnesota

Fact Finders is published by Capstone Press,
151 Good Counsel Drive, P.O. Box 669, Mankato, Minnesota 56002.
www.capstonepress.com

Library of Congress Cataloging-in-Publication Data
Sherman, Josepha.
    Geothermal power / by Josepha Sherman.
    p. cm.—(Fact finders. Energy at work)
    Summary: Introduces the history, uses, production, advantages and disadvantages,
and future of geothermal energy as a power resource.
    Includes bibliographical references and index.
    ISBN 0-7368-2471-5 (hardcover)
    ISBN 0-7368-5191-7 (paperback)
    1. Geothermal resources—Juvenile literature. [1. Geothermal resources.]
I. Title. II. Series.
GB1199.5.S48 2004
333.8'8—dc22
           2003012917

Editorial Credits

Christopher Harbo, editor; Juliette Peters, series designer; Molly Nei, illustrator;
    Alta Schaffer, photo researcher; Eric Kudalis, product planning editor

Photo Credits

Cover: Geothermal power plant in Svartsvehing, Iceland, Corbis/Bob Krist

AP Photo/Eric Risberg, 14–15; Corbis/Bettmann, 10–11; Corbis/Charles O'Rear, 12;
Corbis/Hans Strand, 20–21; Corbis/James A. Sugar, 8; Corbis/Lowell Georgia, 24–25;
Getty Images Inc./David McNew/Newsmakers, 22; Houserstock/Dave G. Houser, 1;
Jeff Henry/Roche Jaune Pictures Inc., 4–5, 9; Leonard Gordon/Root Resources, 13;
NREL/David Parsons, 16; NREL/Joel Renner/INEEL, 19; NREL/Ken Williams/Lawrence
Berkeley Lab, 27; NREL/Warren Gretz, 17, 23; PhotoDisc Inc., 7 (Earth)

1 2 3 4 5 6 09 08 07 06 05 04

Table of Contents

Chapter 1

Old Faithful

On a bright morning, 200 people gather near a small hill covered with white rock. Some people sit on wooden benches. Others stand with their cameras ready. They all watch steam rising from the hill.

Minutes pass. People talk softly as they wait. Then, they hear gurgling. Hot water bubbles from the ground. The crowd grows quiet. Suddenly, a 150-foot (46-meter) fountain shoots into the air. Cameras click, and children squeal. The Old Faithful **geyser** has made its regular appearance again.

Every day, thousands of people watch Old Faithful at Yellowstone National Park. The park is located in Idaho, Montana, and Wyoming.

Old Faithful is one of more than 10,000 geothermal features in Yellowstone National Park. Every day geysers, hot springs, and mud pots show visitors the power of geothermal energy.

Chapter 2

Geothermal Heat

Two ancient Greek words make the word "geothermal." "Geo" means Earth. "Therme" means heat. Geothermal means "heat from the Earth". Geothermal power is energy created from Earth's heat.

Layers of the Earth

Earth is made up of three layers. They are the **crust,** the **mantle,** and the **core.** The crust covers the outside of Earth. It is made of rock and dirt. The mantle is a thick layer of rock. It lies 3 to 35 miles (5 to 56 kilometers) below the crust. The core is a two-part layer about 4,000 miles (6,400 kilometers) below the crust. It is made mainly of iron.

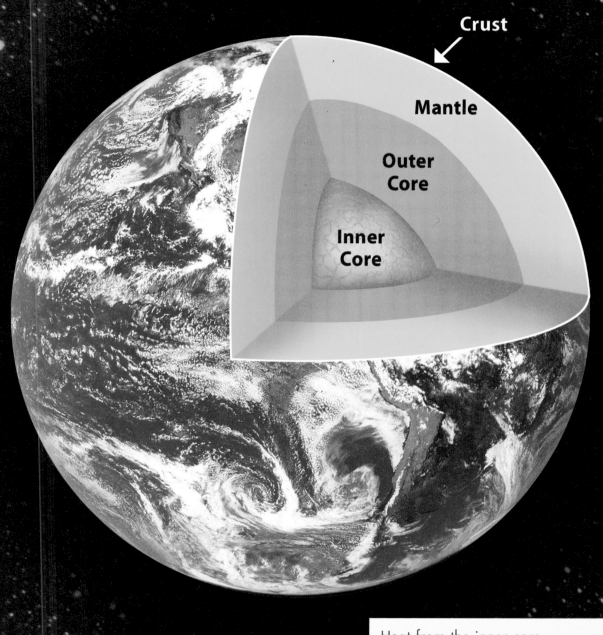

Crust

Mantle

Outer Core

Inner Core

Heat from the inner core rises through Earth's layers.

Rising Heat

Earth's core is superhot. The temperature of the core averages 12,600 degrees Fahrenheit (7,000 degrees Celsius). The core heats the mantle. Some of the mantle's rock melts. This melted rock is called **magma**. The magma rises through the mantle. It moves toward Earth's crust.

Earth's crust is made up of plates. These plates are like giant puzzle pieces. Magma can push through spots along the edge of a plate. Volcanoes form in places where magma breaks through Earth's crust.

Lava flows down the Puu Oo Crater on the island of Hawaii.

Steam rises from the Glory Pool hot spring at Yellowstone National Park.

Most magma stays under the crust. Some of the magma pushes up through cracks in the crust. It heats water and rock deep under ground. The water sometimes reaches the surface. It forms hot springs or geysers like Old Faithful. Most of the water stays below ground. It collects to make geothermal **reservoirs**.

Chapter 3

History of Geothermal Power

People have used geothermal energy for thousands of years. People in North America used hot springs for bathing and cooking 10,000 years ago. Two thousand years ago, Romans in Pompeii built water pipes under their homes. Hot spring water flowed through the pipes to warm their homes.

The Geothermal Industry

In 1913, the first geothermal power plant made electricity in Larderello, Italy. By 1943, the plant made enough electricity for about 130,000 homes.

Tall cooling towers stand above the world's first geothermal power plant in Larderello, Italy.

11

▲ Steam rises from a power plant's cooling towers in The Geysers geothermal field.

FACT!

District heating systems have been used in the United States since the late 1800s. These systems heat groups of homes or businesses. They use water from a hot spring or a geothermal well.

In 1921, John D. Grant built the first geothermal power plant in the United States. He built it in a geothermal field called The Geysers in northern California. Grant's plant made electricity for an area resort.

In 1960, Pacific Gas and Electric began making electricity at The Geysers. Today, power plants at The Geysers produce almost 1,100 **megawatts** of electricity. They bring power to more than 1 million Californians.

At least 20 countries now use geothermal energy. Together, they make about 8,000 megawatts of electricity. Geothermal power is Iceland's second largest energy source. About 85 percent of the homes in Iceland are heated with geothermal energy.

Long pipes carry steam across the Wairakei Geothermal Field in New Zealand. ➤

Chapter 4

Geothermal Power Plants

Geothermal power plants use steam to make electricity. Steam pushes the blades of a **turbine**. The turbine spins to run a **generator**. The generator makes electricity.

Three types of power plants turn geothermal energy into electricity. They are dry steam, flash, and binary power plants.

A worker looks at a generator at the Calpine Sonoma dry steam geothermal plant in Middletown, California.

Dry Steam Power Plants

Many of the first geothermal power plants were dry steam plants. These plants use geothermal reservoirs with a great deal of steam. The steam is piped directly into the turbine to run the generator.

Steam is cooled after it passes through the turbine. The steam turns back into water. The water is pumped down to the reservoir. The water is heated again to make more steam.

FACT!

Power plants at The Geysers use the dry steam method to make electricity.

Large pipes connect condensers to the cooling towers of a power plant at The Geysers. The condensers turn steam ▼ into water.

▲ Generators make electricity at The Leathers flash power plant.
The Leathers is in the Salton Sea geothermal area in California.

Flash Power Plants

Flash power plants use water-filled geothermal reservoirs with little steam. The water in the reservoirs is hot enough to boil. But it is under great pressure. The pressure stops the water from boiling.

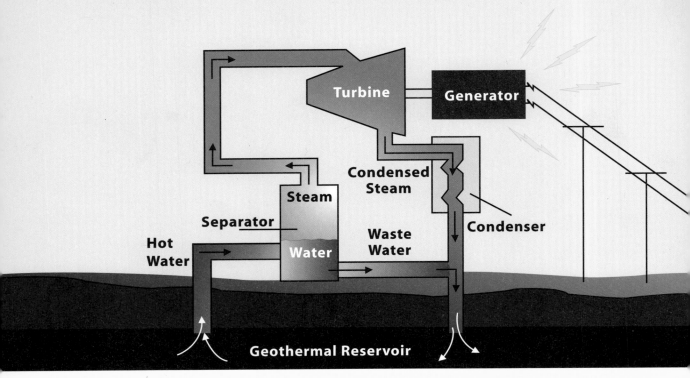

Turbine

Generator

Condensed Steam

Steam

Separator

Condenser

Hot Water

Water

Waste Water

Geothermal Reservoir

▲ Flash power plants turn hot water into steam.

Flash power plants lower the pressure to turn the hot water into steam. The water is pumped into a separator tank. In this low-pressure tank, some of the water "flashes" into steam. The steam turns the turbines and creates electricity. Waste water is pumped back into the ground.

Binary Power Plants

Binary power plants use cooler geothermal reservoirs than flash power plants. Still, the water is quite hot.

Binary plants use hot water to heat a chemical liquid. This liquid boils more easily than water. It turns into a **vapor** when heated with geothermal water. The vapor turns the turbine to create electricity.

Binary plants reuse the water and chemical vapor. The water is pumped back into the well. The vapor is cooled and turned back into a liquid.

F A C T !

In Klamath Falls, Oregon, pipes carry geothermal water under roads and sidewalks. The hot water keeps ice off the roads and sidewalks in winter.

The Wineagle geothermal plant in Wendel-Amedee, California, ▼ is a binary power plant.

19

Chapter 5

Benefits and Drawbacks

Geothermal water can be used over and over again. Steam and water taken out of a reservoir can be pumped back into it. Earth can reheat the water. The water can be used again. But like any form of energy, geothermal power has both benefits and drawbacks.

Benefits

Geothermal energy is a good source of power because it creates little pollution. Dry steam and flash power plants release only low levels of harmful gases such as carbon dioxide.

People swim in the Blue Lagoon hot spring near a geothermal plant in Grindavik, Iceland.

21

Binary power plants release almost no pollution. The plants reuse water and chemicals instead of releasing them into the air.

People can depend on geothermal energy. Geothermal power plants can make electricity 24 hours a day. The energy source is located right below the power plant. Earth never stops heating the reservoirs.

Geothermal power plants can make electricity night and day.

Drawbacks

Geothermal power plants cost a great deal of money to build. Electric companies must spend millions of dollars to find and drill geothermal wells. Each power plant needs many wells to operate and make money.

In many parts of the world, geothermal reservoirs are too far underground to use. They lie under miles of hard rock. Utility companies would need to spend too much money to reach them.

▲ A drilling rig drills a geothermal well in Imperial Valley, California.

FACT!

Some geothermal reservoirs release a chemical called hydrogen sulphide (H_2S). It smells like rotten eggs. Some power plants are able to remove H_2S from geothermal steam.

Chapter 6

The Future

Geothermal power has a promising future. It creates enough electricity to power 3.5 million homes in the United States. It makes about 7 percent of California's electricity. In years to come, scientists hope to create more energy from geothermal heat.

Drilling deeper into Earth may be the key to using more geothermal energy. Most dry rock about 5 to 10 miles (8 to 16 kilometers) below Earth's surface is hot enough to create energy. Engineers are studying ways to reach this rock.

A drilling rig drills a new steam
well at a geothermal power plant
near Geyserville, California.

Engineers are working to find ways to drill deeper than they are now. Once wells are drilled, engineers want to pour cold water down to the hot rock. The water would heat up and be pumped back out to make electricity. With deep enough wells, geothermal power could be used anywhere in the world.

Geothermal power promises to be an important source of energy for the future. In time, coal, oil, and natural gas will become harder to find. People will need to use other sources of power. Geothermal power may become one of the world's most important sources of energy.

Engineers run tests on a geothermal rig in Soultz, France. They are studying ways to use heat from hot, dry rock deep below Earth's surface. ➡

Fast Facts

- Yellowstone National Park has about 10,000 geothermal features.

- Geothermal means "heat from the Earth" in the ancient Greek language.

- The average temperature of Earth's core is about 12,600 degrees Fahrenheit (7,000 degrees Celsius).

- In 1913, the world's first geothermal power plant began making electricity in Larderello, Italy.

- Power plants at The Geysers in northern California make electricity for more than 1 million people each year.

- Geothermal energy is used to make about 8,000 megawatts of electricity around the world.

- The three types of geothermal power plants are dry steam, flash, and binary power plants.

Hands On: Make a Turbine

Geothermal power plants use steam to make electricity. Try this activity to see how steam is used to turn turbines.

What You Need
teakettle filled with water
stove
adult
pinwheel

What You Do
1. Place a teakettle filled with water on the stove top.
2. Ask an adult to turn on the burner and boil the water.
3. When steam starts coming out of the teakettle's spout, put the front of the pinwheel in the steam. Keep your hand away from the steam. It could burn your skin.

What happened when the steam hit the blades of the pinwheel? When the steam from a geothermal reservoir enters a turbine, the turbine spins. The spinning turbine runs a generator that makes electricity.

Glossary

core (KOR)—the inner part of Earth that is made of metal, rocks, and melted rock

crust (KRUHST)—the thin outer layer of Earth's surface

generator (JEN-uh-ray-tur)—a machine that makes electricity by turning a magnet inside a coil of wire

geyser (GYE-zur)—an underground spring that shoots hot water and steam through a hole in the ground

magma (MAG-muh)—melted rock beneath Earth's crust

mantle (MAN-tuhl)—the layer of melted rock that surrounds Earth's core

megawatt (MEG-uh-wot)—a unit for measuring electrical power; one megawatt is the rate at which about 1,000 homes use power.

reservoir (REZ-ur-vwar)—a natural or artificial holding area for large amounts of water or steam

turbine (TUR-bine)—an engine powered by water, steam, or gas moving through the blades of a fan

vapor (VAY-pur)—a gas made from something that is usually a liquid or solid at normal temperatures

Internet Sites

FactHound offers a safe, fun way to find Internet sites related to this book. All of the sites on FactHound have been researched by our staff.

Here's how:

1. Visit *www.facthound.com*
2. Type in this special code **0736824715** for age-appropriate sites. Or enter a search word related to this book for a more general search.
3. Click on the Fetch It button.

FactHound will fetch the best sites for you!

Read More

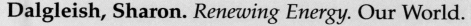

Dalgleish, Sharon. *Renewing Energy.* Our World. Philadelphia: Chelsea House, 2003.

Graf, Mike. *Yellowstone National Park.* National Parks. Mankato, Minn.: Bridgestone Books, 2003.

Morgan, Sally. *Alternative Energy Sources.* Science at the Edge. Chicago: Heinemann Library, 2003.

Snedden, Robert. *Energy Alternatives.* Essential Energy. Chicago: Heinemann Library, 2002.

Index